Curious Kids Guides
LONG AGO

Philip Steele

KINGFISHER

NEW YORK

LONG AGO

KINGFISHER
Larousse Kingfisher Chambers Inc.
80 Maiden Lane
New York, New York 10038
www.kingfisherpub.com

First published in 1994
First published in this format 2002
10 9 8 7 6 5 4 3 2 1
1TR/1201/TIMS/*UD UNV/128MA

LIBRARY OF CONGRESS CATALOGING-IN-PUBLICATION DATA
has been applied for.

ISBN 0-7534-5469-6

Printed in China

Series editor: Jackie Gaff
Series designer: David West Children's Books
Author: Philip Steele
Editor: Brigid Avison
Art Editor: Christina Fraser
Main illustrations: Chris Forsey 4-5; Terry Gabbey (Eva Morris) 8-9, 12-13;
Nick Harris (Virgil Pomfret Agency) 6-7, 14-17, 24-25; Adam Hook (Linden
Artists) 22-23; Christa Hook (Linden Artists) 10-11; David Mitcheson 18,
30-31; Nicki Palin 20-21, 28; Tony Smith (Virgil Pomfret Agency) 26-27.
Inset illustrations: Chris Forsey 4tl, 5bl, 21t; Stephen Holmes 19, 23tr;
Adam Hook (Linden Artists) 6tl, 10tl, 14tl, 15mr; 16tl, 20tl, 22tl, 22tr,
23m, 24tl, 25tr, 26tlml, 30tl; Tony Kenyon (B.L.Kearley) all cartoons;
Nicky Palin27br; Ross Watton (Garden Studio) 28tl, 29ml.

CONTENTS

What were the Middle Ages in the middle of?

We call the years between the ancient world and the modern world in Europe the Middle Ages. They started in the 470s, when rule by the Romans came to an end, and they ended in the 1450s.

NORTH AMERICA

Newfoundlar

IROQUOIS

ANASAZI

Pueblo Bonito

ATLANTIC OCEAN

MAYA

AZTECS

SOUTH AMERICA

INCAS

PACIFIC OCEAN

• The Romans once ruled most of Europe and North Africa. Then fierce warriors invaded, splitting Roman lands into many small kingdoms. By the 1450s Europe had larger countries again, more like those of today.

• The map above includes the people and places talked about in this book.

• In the Middle Ages, no one knew what the whole world looked like.

VIKINGS

ASIA

EUROPE

JAPAN

MONGOLS

Venice

PERSIA

CHINA

Leshan

Mediterranean
Sea

INDIA

Angkor
Wat

Fez

ARABIA

Timbuktu

AFRICA

Ife

INDIAN
OCEAN

AUSTRALIA

Great
Zimbabwe

NEW ZEALAND

MAORIS

● This is what Arab mapmakers thought the world looked like in the 1150s. It shows Asia, North Africa, and Europe. Neither the Arabs nor the Europeans knew about other parts of the world.

● Most people thought the world was flat. Sailors had to be brave to go on long voyages — they were afraid of falling over the edge!

Why did kings and queens wear crowns?

Rulers had much more power in the Middle Ages than they do today. They made the laws, and everyone had to do what they said. A glittering golden crown was like a badge — it was one way of showing how important the king or queen was.

- In many countries today, laws are made by a group of people chosen by all the people.

Barons and bishops

King and queen

Knights

Freemen and women

Peasants

- The king told the barons what to do. The barons told the knights what to do. Everyone told the poor peasants what to do.

- The ruler of the Inca people of South America was called the Sapa Inca. His crown was made of gold and feathers. His tunic and cloak were made of fine wool.

Why were the peasants revolting?

Well, they didn't actually look revolting, just a bit muddy! Poor people often rose up in revolt and fought against their rulers, though. They were trying to win a better way of life.

- The peasants had to give money or food to their local lord every year — even though they often went hungry themselves.

- European kings and queens were often given funny nicknames. Some rulers were good, some were bad — and some were just ugly!

Malcolm the Bighead
King of Scotland

Wladislaw the Short
King of Poland

Emanuel the Happy
King of Portugal

Why did castles have moats?

Moats were deep wide ditches filled with water, which made it harder for enemies to break into a castle. Friendly visitors could cross the moat over a drawbridge. But when enemies attacked, the drawbridge was raised.

● Spies and traitors were chained up in the castle's dungeons. These were dark and damp and full of rats and spiders!

● One way to beat enemies who shut themselves up in a castle was to surround it — and wait! This was called a siege. When the castle ran out of food and water, the people inside had to give in.

● Strong stone walls were built to protect towns and cities all over the world. The picture on the right shows Great Zimbabwe, a walled city begun in the 1000s by the Shona people of southern Africa.

● Pueblo Bonito was one of the walled towns built by the Anasazi people of North America between 950 and 1300.

● In the 1300s, people in Europe learned how to make big guns called cannons. In time it became easier to blow up castles — if the guns went off properly!

Why did knights wear armor?

In battle, knights were bashed and battered by swords, arrows, axes, long pointed lances, and metal clubs called maces. They had to protect their bodies from all these sharp weapons, so they wore suits of tough metal armor.

● Until the 1200s most knights wore chainmail armor. This was made from linked metal rings. Later armor was made from solid metal plates.

By the end of the Middle Ages, a knight was like a can of beans on legs completely covered with metal!

● Putting on armor wasn't easy. A squire was a boy who was learning to be a knight. He helped the knight get ready for battle.

Armor wasn't very comfortable to wear, so knights put on thick padded clothes underneath.

● Japanese knights were called samurai. Their armor was made of metal plates attached to padded silk and leather.

● Bows and deadly arrows were used by soldiers in most parts of the world.

Welsh longbowman

Turkish crossbowman

Aztec warrior

Mongol archer

● A samurai always had a bath before going into battle. Then, if he died, he knew he would be clean and ready to go to heaven.

Why did churches have steeples?

Steeples made churches look as if they were pointing up to heaven. During the Middle Ages, people throughout the world showed love for their god by building beautiful churches, mosques, or temples.

● Even church roofs and drainpipes were decorated, sometimes with very ugly heads called gargoyles. Rainwater spouted out through their mouths.

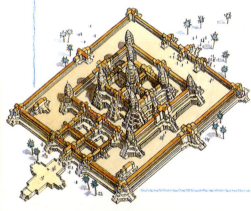

● The world's biggest holy building is the Hindu temple of Angkor Wat, in Cambodia. It was built in the 1100s. You could fit 8,317 tennis courts inside it!

● Spire builders worked high above the ground on a tiny wooden platform. It must have been very dangerous!

Why did mosques have minarets?

Minarets are the tall slender towers on mosques, the buildings where Muslims pray to God. They, too, point to heaven. At the top of the minaret is a balcony, where a man called a muezzin stands to call people to prayer.

● In 803, workers finished carving a 230-foot-high statue of Buddha into cliffs near the town of Leshan, in China. Two people can sit on just one of its toenails! Gautama Buddha was a great religious teacher who was born in India in the 560s B.C.

Who wore steeples on their heads?

All kinds of weird and wonderful headdresses passed in and out of fashion in Europe during the Middle Ages. In the 1400s women began wearing tall hats called hennins, which looked a little like church steeples. Getting through a doorway must have been tricky — some hennins were nearly 3 feet high!

● There weren't shops selling ready-made clothes. Rich people paid tailors to make their clothes. Poor people made their own.

● Some hats were shaped like animals' horns. Others were like butterflies' wings.

- People showed off all their money by wearing expensive clothes and jewelry. The finest materials were made in Italy, Spain, and the East.

- Some French knights trying to escape from an enemy army had to cut the points off their shoes before they could run away!

- Have you ever seen shoes with long pointed toes like this? The toes were so long they had to be tied to the wearer's leg! They were all the rage for men about 600 years ago.

Who wore platform shoes?

Streets were so muddy that noble women started to wear shoes with very high soles. Maids often had to hold the lady up as she walked along!

Why did people eat with their fingers?

Although Europeans used knives and spoons at mealtimes, no one had forks. Rich and poor alike put pieces of food into their mouths with their fingers instead. At feasts, servants passed around fish and meat in handy chunks, so they were easy to pick up — if they weren't covered with slippery sauce!

● Town water was usually dirty and full of germs, so it was lucky most people drank wine or ale!

● It was good manners to throw leftover bones onto the floor for the dogs.

● A royal feast might end with a giant surprise pie. When the pie was opened, out would jump musicians, acrobats, or strange animals.

● Until the 1400s, most people didn't eat off plates. They used a thick slice of bread called a trencher instead — sometimes finishing their meal by eating it.

Who first grew potatoes?

The people of South America grew and ate potatoes, but until the 1500s no one else had ever seen a potato, let alone tasted one! Explorers took these and many other new vegetables to Europe from the Americas.

● Poor peasants had little choice of food. Most ate dark bread made of rye or barley flour, porridge, or vegetable stews.

● The Incas of South America kept a kind of guinea pig for food, just as farmers in other countries kept pigs. Guinea pigs are still eaten in Peru today.

Who was first to chew gum?

The Maya people of Central America chewed a rubbery gum they called chicle. They collected it from the sapodilla tree.

What were garderobes?

Castle toilets were called garderobes. They were usually built high up in the walls. Everything fell down into the moat, or into a stinky cesspool — which some unlucky servant had to clean out from time to time.

● There weren't many toilets in the Middle Ages. Most town people used pots, and just poured the smelly contents away into the street.

Did people take baths?

People around the world had different ideas about bathing, but it wasn't too popular with Europeans at this time. People who had money could pay to visit a public bathhouse. Only the very rich had their own bathtubs. They used wooden tubs, so they had to watch out for splinters!

● Southern Europeans started using soap in the 700s. It took a bit longer for northerners to start washing behind their ears!

This is what a plague flea looks like magnified 15 times under a microscope.

● The Black Death began in about 1338 and spread from Asia to Europe, carried by rats. The rats had tiny fleas, which passed the plague on when they bit people.

What was the Black Death?

The Black Death was the kind of terrible sickness we call a plague. Within just 13 years, it killed at least one out of every three people in Asia and Europe. Whole families and villages were wiped out.

Did children have to go to school?

There weren't many schools in the Middle Ages, and most children never went to one. Sometimes, schools were run by a church, mosque, or temple. Children went mainly to learn about religion. Only a few were taught to read and write.

● Some boys and a few girls were sent away to learn a trade, such as being a butcher or a wool seller. They were called apprentices.

● Students have been going to the University of Karueein, at Fez in Morocco, since the year 859.

● Although very few girls went to school, there were some famous women writers. Christine de Pisan of France lived in the 1400s. She was one of the first people to write about ways of making women's lives better.

ROMAN	I	II	III	IV	V	VI	VII	VIII	IX	X
HINDI (INDIA)	۱	۲	۳	۴	۵	۶	۷	۸	۹	۱۰
MODERN ARABIC	۱	۲	۳	۴	۵	۶	۷	۸	۹	۱۰
MEDIEVAL EUROPEAN	I	2	3	8	4	6	Λ	8	9	10
MODERN	1	2	3	4	5	6	7	8	9	10

● In the early 1400s, 2,000 Chinese scholars wrote the biggest encyclopedia ever known. It had 22,937 chapters! Even if you read a chapter a day, it would take you over 60 years to finish it.

● The Arabs wrote their numbers in a way that had begun in India. European scholars began to copy them, and gave up using the old Roman numbers.

Why did Incas get tied up in knots?

The Inca people didn't have a written language. Instead they had long colored strings which they called quipus. These were tied into knots to count and remember things.

● Only a few noble Inca children were taught the secret of how to use a quipu. Today, even the brainiest scientists have gotten tied up in knots trying to crack the code!

Why were books chained up?

Books were rare because each one had to be written out slowly by hand. Until the 1400s, there were no machines to print them quickly. This made the books very precious, so they were often chained up to keep people from stealing them.

● Monks made books, writing with goose quills dipped in ink. They spent many hours decorating each page, using bright colors and even tiny slivers of gold.

● The Chinese were the first people to print books rather than copy them by hand, about 1,300 years ago. They used wooden blocks.

● In Europe, printing began when a German called Johann Gutenberg built a printing press in the 1440s. He used metal type blocks.

Why was it hard to tell the time?

There were clocks that told the time by drips of water, but they froze over in winter. There were candles that told the time as they slowly burned down, but they kept blowing out. And there were sundials that used shadows to tell the time — except when it was cloudy!

● Thank heavens they finally invented clocks that went tick-tock! These were kept going by weights and gearwheels.

Gearwheel

Weight

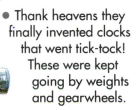

● Spinning wheels came to Europe from China and India in about 1200. Like all good inventions, they made life better — turning a wheel to spin thread was much easier and quicker than twiddling a spindle.

● Europeans first built windmills to grind their flour in the late 1100s. Persians had already been using them for hundreds of years.

Where did china come from?

From China, of course! Pottery was made all over the world, but the very finest was invented in southern China. It is called porcelain.

● It was probably a Venetian workman making glass windows who discovered that pieces of glass could help people with poor eyesight to see better.

What blew up in Venice?

Venice was famous for its glass, which is made by melting sand and other materials. It is shaped while it is still hot and soft. Glassblowers blow it up like a balloon, through a long iron tube.

● The Chimú people of South America used precious gold and turquoise to make this knife. In the 1400s, Chimú lands were taken over by the Incas.

● The Yoruba people were brilliant metalworkers who lived in the kingdom of Ife, in West Africa. This bronze sculpture was made in the 1300s and shows the head of a king.

Why did artists paint with eggs?

There weren't shops selling tubes of paint in the Middle Ages, so artists had to make their own. In Europe they made a kind of paint called tempera by mixing egg yolks and water into their colors.

Why was soccer banned?

Soccer wasn't played on a field in the Middle Ages — boys just chased the ball through the streets, yelling and kicking and knocking people over. By 1314, it had got so bad that King Edward II of England banned the sport in London.

• Soccer balls were made from pigs' bladders.

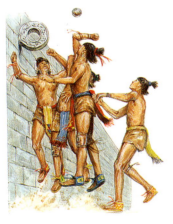

• The Aztecs and the Maya played a game called tlachtli, with a rubber ball on a stone court. It was a little like basketball.

• Lacrosse was first played by the Iroquois people of North America. Games could last for hours, with as many as 1,000 people in each team!

What was the Festival of Fools?

The Festival of Fools was held in many parts of Europe around Christmas time. It was a kind of holiday, when ordinary people had fun pretending to be lords and priests, and doing all kinds of silly or naughty things.

Who said yes to Nō plays?

Nō are Japanese plays in which actors wear masks and move very slowly, telling story-poems through mime and dance. They were first performed in the 1300s, at the court of the Japanese emperor.

Where was Vinland?

Viking sailors from Scandinavia were the first Europeans to cross the Atlantic Ocean and reach North America. They landed on the east coast in the early 1000s and named it Vinland, or Vineland, because they found lots of grapevines there.

● No one is quite certain where Vinland was, but the most likely place is Newfoundland, in what is Canada today. People now think the Vikings found cranberries or gooseberries there, not grapes!

Who went to sea in junks?

By the 1400s, Chinese junks were the world's biggest ships. The largest were five times the size of ships being built in Europe.

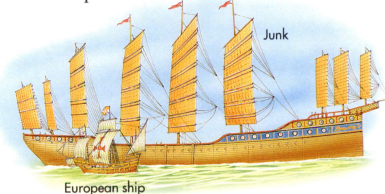

Junk

European ship

● A Moroccan called Ibn Batuta spent 30 years traveling. He went east to India, China, and Sumatra, and south to Timbuktu, in Africa. He lived in the 1300s.

● One of the great explorers of the Middle Ages was a Venetian named Marco Polo. It took him four whole years to travel to China.

● Polynesian sailors explored the vast South Pacific Ocean in nothing bigger than canoes. The Maoris are descended from Polynesians who reached New Zealand about 1,000 years ago.

Was Sinbad a real sailor?

The exciting adventures of Sinbad the Sailor were folktales made up by Persian storytellers in the Middle Ages. Although Sinbad was make-believe, there were lots of real people making amazing journeys over land and across the ocean.

Where did Robin Hood live?

The stories about Robin Hood say he lived in Sherwood Forest, near the English town of Nottingham. He and his Merry Men were outlaws, because they broke the law by robbing the rich, but they gave the money to poor people.

● Was there really such a person as Robin Hood? Nobody knows for sure. Some people think he was an outlaw called Robert Fitzooth, the Earl of Huntingdon.

● People have told stories about Robin Hood, Maid Marian, and the Merry Men since the 1300s.

● Everyone enjoys a good story. Today we can look at books or watch movies and videos. In the Middle Ages, people loved to listen to storytellers.

Who was Joan of Arc?

Joan was a French peasant girl who grew up at a time when England and France were at war. In 1429, at the age of 17, she dressed up as a soldier and helped to free the city of Orleans from an English army. But just a year later she was captured and burned at the stake.

Who was a teenage warrior?

Temujin was the son of a leader of the Mongol people of central Asia. He was born in 1162 and he became a warrior when he was only 13, after his father died. He took the name Genghis Khan. Under his leadership, the Mongols attacked and won many lands in Asia.